MY CONVICTIONS

(A BOOK OF LIFE, LOVE AND SPIRITUAL CONVICTIONS)

Hamilton Walker

authorHOUSE®

AuthorHouse™ LLC
1663 Liberty Drive
Bloomington, IN 47403
www.authorhouse.com
Phone: 1-800-839-8640

Published by AuthorHouse   04/02/2014

ISBN: 978-1-4969-0015-9 (sc)
ISBN: 978-1-4969-0014-2 (e)

Library of Congress Control Number: 2014905737

Any people depicted in stock imagery provided by Thinkstock are models, and such images are being used for illustrative purposes only.
Certain stock imagery © Thinkstock.

This book is printed on acid-free paper.

Contents

Forward..vii

Poetry of Life, Love and Spirituality

Reality Check 3
Fancy Queen 6
Hocus-Pocus...8
The Harvest 10
Pushed 12
Old Glory.. 13
Stand Fast...15
Conception 16
Rise Again 18
A Freshly Painted Picture 19
Exposure...22
My Conviction...24
Lotus...25
Omnipotent...26

Convictions

Life Convictions 27
Love Conviction 43
Spiritual Conviction....................................47

Biography

This page is dedicated to Janie Fulton who helped me make all the other pages possible.

Forward

This book is written to be intruding and entertaining. The reader will find it cries with the reality of life. The author uses his imagination to throw light in dark areas with spiritual and storytelling poems that have a unique rhythm. It is through expressing his emotional ties with poetry that he is able to quite his mind and tries to disentangle the knots of life.

Poetry of Life, Love and Spirituality

Reality Check

Please do not disturb the baby.
Put more money in the pot.
Opportunities are in the dividends.
At the scene of the crime is a live wire.
This message will be recorded for
training purposes.
Anticipate the backyard slide with a zoom
lens. Evolution has invaded the integrity of
the righteous.
Please hold for the next available operator.
This message is being recorded for training
purposes.
Peeping Tom's uncle is telling part of the truth
to the digital nation.
It happens every day.
Put in a little and get a lot.
Hit the jack pot.
It is a billion dollar scam.
It only works for those who are standing at the
top.
The accuser will not be accused for the crime
that opposed the people.
They arrested the innocent because it was
registered to the owner.
The guiltless pays for crimes that someone
else has committed.

This is no deception and it is not
happening ten thousand miles away.
The joy sticks are not lollipops for the all
night suckers.
How many licks do it takes to get to the
center of...
Please fill in the blank; Name, Age, Sex, and
Race.
It's not a stolen identity.
They have the people at the tip of their finger.
Program, program gets with their program.
It's a game of chance.
Plug in a number and pull the level.
Don't adjust the picture.
You are now being taken control of.
The videos are real time.
Pedestrians don't think, it is serious, or fail
to realize.
They are being watched like celebrities.
The camera creates the illusion of the
truth. The big screen captures everything
in living color.
Entertain yourself; get your popcorn and
brandy.
The metric system is in a standard world.
A multi-billion dollar dream must explode to
hit the mark.
Don't worry because they will get it right.

Gun shots are now being heard from a switch
board.
An optic lens is on every street corner.
Surveillance captures the line of fire in the
middle of the war.
Who is committing the crime that keeps
making a paperless trail?
If, the gloves don't fit, we must acquit.
Pardon me, for the pardon you gave was not
yours to give.
One way or another reality will prevail.

Fancy Queen

Fiddler crabs wave with the merge of the surf
Rollers pull and push the shore line
the sky sprinkles glitter in the dawn
Refreshing the folds of paradise crystalline
jewels cling to the tips of each tongue
Vibrant treasure absorbing the diluted bliss
Liquid sunshine saturates the thirst and
widens the central perception
Dole by the vim of natures charm
Sand Piper scroll the edge of the foamy brew
pacing for the morsel of life
A distant sail swells the surging breath of
serenity
penetrating boundless destinies
She leans forward and drenches me with
fantasy
Vibrant sparkles dazzle her brow
Mesmerized by her beauty
a golden goddess placed on a mantel whisked
fully masked
Forbearance is her nature
she ministers the wind of pleasure
Pulling my string like a puppeteer I paid
Desiring her every move
I gave her my all
A clam lulled her, as her mask wrinkled
a drift

Days floating in her faith
She blew a kiss from the palm of her heart
Unfolding...pudendum like a flower
Charming and soothing sounds expanded the
sheets
As they glide across the breast
I dare not tread in the shallow water that runs
across her cheeks
Or dredge the scars of her past
Feeling the firmness of her frame
I took her with the grip of my soul
to be forever lost in her bosom
Nurturing... The ebullience of my being

Hocus-Pocus

Broken glass and cigarettes butts lay on the metro.
A cardboard mommy sleeps by the warm sewer drain.
A speeding vehicle with flashing red lights screamed at the pedestrians.
The sounds unravel old news, and awaken the dead.
Crawling from the sewer like a cockroach, a spirit peeps at the world.
The tattered soul takes a sip from the flask to pacify the demons.
Knit, or weave a white or blue collar.
One size fits all.
It's not contagious if… you keep your distance.
Everyone carries their own survival kit.
The grocery carts move the destitute.
Whose love has forsaken them?
A tailor waits with black and white textile.
Doctors do not make street calls.
The paramedic rushes to the scene to pour salt into sore eyes.
Crunch the numbers, and roll out the welcome mat.
It is time to vote.

The magicians beautify the city with makeup
and sweepers.
The city sweepers clean up the city, by pushing
trash under the rug.
Hope is a broken promise.
No one can see them crying.
They are drowning in their own tears.
No one can see them dying or thinking about
the time.
Our prayers bring the demons home.
The journalist's shine their shameful lime light,
on the city's new construction.
All it takes is love to cure the infection.
They let the wounded fester, and raise the
price of the living.
So... only the rich can afford it.
Go to the back of the line and start over.
Read the fine print.
One will find, there is no compensation for
purple hearts.
It is too late, when red tape is circled with
white chalk.
Pay attention to the protocol, as they play leap
frog with the souls of the freedom fighters.

The Harvest

Turn on the red lights.
The stage is smoking.
The hazed neon lights filter reality.
They looked for the stars in the clouds.
Let the D.J. play the nostalgic music that
intoxicates memories.
She floats out slowly luring their hearts into
her spells.
Gentlemen laughter and stale perfume
surrounded her.
She shakes her cookie to antagonize their
spirits.
They shout, "let it rain!"
Green leaves fall freely through the clouds.
Some reach out and donate to a charitable
cause.
Her door is open for request.
She squats on anyone's
fantasy. She got skills like a
cowboy.
Wet dreams and whiskey makes their cash flow
freely.
Her dehydrated misfortunes keep her dancing.

Slang shot virtues and stretch marked dreams
are frozen in a made up smile.
No prince has come to claim her baggage.
She closes her eyes and dances.
Are there any more requests?
She is a late harvest.

Sky rise tilted statutes
rooted heart
municipality transfuse micro plasma
debilitated creed
Forged shields fused
Experience Callous
Bonds dislocate harmony
Monolithic principles
Solidified words cut mercy
Premeditated assumption
blankets relationships
Mechanized Frolic
electrified stimulant
Skinner's box
Button

PUSHED

Old Glory

Independence is freedom.
Leave your possessions.
Promise…
Step in and sign on the dotted line. Promises…
Finance your dreams and travel the world.
Promise to come back.
Your love is now memories.
Shiny boots, cadence songs at the break of
dawn.
Who's your momma?
Recondition
Who's your daddy?
Condition
Meat and potatoes Program
Fit in or, kicked out
Stand at your post soldier and secure those
orders.
Challenge the world; no one can enter without
a pass.
Hold on to those virtues of peace.
Step and turn… for the world can see, step and
turn on point.
Dress right dress to the cadence.
…Old Glory

Gracefully marching to Zion stand fast to
watch the world.
...Old Glory
Planted high on its countrymen's soil.
Broken and tattered she has fallen to chance.
Stop the raven from demising her in the
streets.
See the faces of death.
Don't let them burn her words of freedom.
Secure your post soldier for
the lamb is covered with blood.
Fertile soil rests the weary.
All that come to battle must pay the price for
freedom.
He who fights for what is right, gains the
sword of truth.
In the winding wall of tyranny the scroll of
freedom is protected.
Peace is never lost. It is only abandoned.

Stand Fast

Stand at your post soldier and secure those orders.
Propaganda halts the friendly and the foe.
He stands tall.
The brass hanging like grapes on his lapel are glowing like diamonds.
Sparkling back leather shoes mirror the sun.
His moves are robotic.
Like a clock he stops and stands fast watching the elements.
Dress right dress to the cadence.
Old glory was planted high on the countryman soil.
Broken and tatter she has fallen in to chance.
Watch them rape her in the streets and burn those words of freedom.
Secure the post my soldiers for there is buffalo to be slaughtered.
Winter comes in summer heat.
Peace welcomes the graveyard.
All that come this way let them see the power.
The might of the right or, the right of the might shall come to past.

Conception

Grace floated in on a heavenly cloud.
The scent of her flower was his temptation in the garden.
A submissive breeze of passion blanketed her heart.
Her emotion was the threshold to life.
Her heart was the catalyst to love.
She completed him.
The creatures of his world had no emotions.
He stood lonely.
No man can sustain himself with loneliness.
Grace was his gift from the havens.
He embraced her cloud, and inhaled her passion.
Her passionate flames burned like the sun.
He impounded her flames, and submitted to her every desire.
Embracing her soul, he submerged in the abyss of temptations.
They were the conception of their father.
He teased them with the substance of the world.
His fruits desired all the flavors in the garden.
They ingested perception.
Their conscious waited the day to be awakened.

Knowledge slumber in ignorance and,
ignorance craves understanding.
Free will is an appetite.
Let it be known.
He had given them the hunger for knowledge.
A secret can only have one master,
and there is only one truth, and it is naked in
the beginning, until... it is covered with
misconceptions.

Rise Again

Rise up falling fighter stand up on your feet
again.
The Noble will twist the philosophy of life by
holding ritual to salvation.
Making the flock think the pleasure of life is a
concept.
Slaughter those who spread the true light.
Pave the way my soldiers give life to the dead.
Mind not your suffering.
Never mind what's been said.
Love can never be destroyed.
See the light shine.
Your seeds have been planted.
Hear love calling.
Let them shackle your hands and legs.
No matter how hard they try,
they cannot shackle your heart.
Let your words be the song of salvation.
Your seeds will not die.
Plant those seeds my brethren.
Hear the sibling crying.
My veterans, take care... The devil is a lie.
Are you listening?

A Freshly Painted Picture

Watch the silhouette fall, target practice for
unmarked graves.
Check its authentic serial number. It's
a collector's item.
Try to swallow the ingested grief and to never
realize that an open hand carries more than
a closed fist.
Watch the jealous contender stock pile
liberation.
Transferring its accounts into another
revelation.
While the proclamation lays dormant.
They rape Mother Nature and cheat Father
Time genuinely engineering immortality with
prefabricated souls.
Read between the lines.
A transfusion of deduction is the answer for
cloning the future and downsizing humanity.
An explanation for spirituality is a Big Bang.
See, the conformation for liberation is the
possession of a weapon of mass destruction.
When it defuses in smaller hands,
it makes the third rock not a planet.
Then, little brother becomes an equal.
That is not the conformation.

Watch fear, greed and destitution fuse a time
bomb and ignorance blind understanding.
Some kind of stranger is working for
justification.
Ruler, champion, icon, mentor at home among
family.
Confused... home is some kind of desolation.
A fish grows not larger than the space it
occupies, corrupted by fixation, quest for
perception.
Pray for forgiveness and never let go old habits.
Caught in the world, never see the flame
growing smaller.
No truths are accepted.
Because ignorance blinds understanding
and the truth is always being over shadowed
by a painted picture,
like over exposed dreams spiraling in
multicolor flowing down the
drain, it becomes one.
See... the impact of the book of knowledge.
It is ever so easy... love and obey.
However, it doesn't connect when the line is
busy.
Tentative understanding is hard to
comprehend.

When... a fetish mind sees through only
one pair of Eyes
and a twisted tongue keeps amending the
truth; that keeps life complicated.
Blindfold justice and balance her hands.

Exposure

On the other side of Eden war is declared on peace.
They inhabit the world with trinkets' and mirrors.
"Gifts from God, "they say.
Buccaneers undress the seasons.
Whispering in gibberish voices, they call her precious
and pick her fruit before it is ripe.
All the trees are timber developing tomorrow's paradise.
Clear the timber and field the grounds.
The cattle graze disappointments, as the soil washes away.
Seeds are now trying to pay for tomorrow's harvest.
Once the ground is tainted nothing will grow.
It's not economical to import the export to survive
Give work to competitions.
Your home land suffers.
Rationalize that...
Hear the bell ringing.
It's time to go or, it is time to come.
Educate the living not the dead.

Will Justice peel her mask and see?
The words are written in blood, or stand
indecisive.
Watch them wash the writing off the wall. My
people fret not the illusions.
Sirens are luring the hopeful in to the rigid
rocks in the swift tides.
Time is winding down.
On the other side of Eden the waters are tainted
with a plague.
So no one can find the purity in the fountain.
Rise up and keep it together.
The whole is greater than the sum.
Let your voices make one sound.
Our savior is not dead.
Embrace the movement.
Yes we can!
Yes we will!
Make a change …

My Conviction

Regular Joe
      conviction
Unattach
      Umbilical
         cord
Living notes
Courage
      Strength
Variability
      Rationality
         Good
         Evil
Love   Spirit   Justifies
Personal Reason
      For Being
      Who
      I am

Beneath

                    the powder blue

Sky, quaalude
colored butterflies foster

and   loosely   around

A Breeze freshly fills the lungs
begins

          the sensuous

                 Journey

Shadow
sunlight

     glaring dormant images

                  Lay

         across

broken ligaments
whose weightless

          footsteps left no
           signs

of a pathway

        A silhouette

  of a body
sits

           asylum peace.

Lotus

Omnipotent

A shallow grave

Living rock

crumbling into dirt

civilization

into dirt

crumbling

Bone

Yard

dusting

prying

scraping

digging

past

Alpha

Justifies

Omega

Life Convictions

Life #1

The influence of One's positive words can radiate the world.

Life #2

Some truths are revealed only to the pure of heart.

Life#3

Some things in life should be left alone. Be careful with your perception. Your eyes can reveal things that may not be true until your psychologist awakes you to reality. The mind should not be taken to the point of no return.

Life#4

Going with the flow has no obstacles. Following your heart has many obstacles. Great things come from great love.

Life#5

Placebos are the cure for those who believe it. The power of acceptance will make life manageable.

Life#6

A feast can only be consumed one bite at a time. Too big of a bite will not allow one to chew or swallow. Take small bites and chew your food slowly, it would make digesting it a lot easier. Even though there are many plates on the table, it is your stomach not your appetite that holds the food

Life#7

What is on one's mind may be the concern of those whom one encounters. One's expressions may not be the world's interpretation if One is waiting for the world to make things better. One will have some time to wait. Many words should be seen and not heard.

Life#8

Wealth is more valuable when it helps the misfortunate. Knowledge is useless if not engaged respectably.

Life#9

One need not be led or followed working with a brother. **UNITY.**

Life#10

People are always looking for imperfection. Don't be disappointed with the criticism, consider the source.

Life#11

Sometimes, One invests too much time gathering misfortunes. One cannot put spilled milk back into the milk bottle for consumption. Many times the greatest gain is in the challenge of letting go of what was lost.

Life#12

Hats have several purposes. The ambience of elements adjusts its position. Humility, patience and understanding are a few attributes of the server. Selfishness, shortcomings, and ignorance can loosely fit their objective. There are those who serve, and those who seize opportunities to make the HAT FIT.

Life#13

"MONEY"
Too little is not enough; too much is a waste.

Life#14

Bigger guns will not solve anything. It only causes bigger casualties.

Life#15

An overripe fruit can be nauseating to the consumer.
Daily News....

Life#16

Don't expect more when, you're giving less.

Life#17

When One has no more secrets, One has no more lies. The truth may not be merciful. Lies have won many battles and lost all respect.

Life#18

Our intentions are different from their observations.

Life#19

"PATIENCE"
 No one can see our vision unless we give them the light. Sometimes people are caught in an illusion of their own perceptions.

Life#20

There are endless shades of colors. Red, white, yellow and green are a few to be seen. When you mix them all together, thcy bccome BLACK.

Life#21

A bigger wager than what One has is gambling it all.

Life#22

Success is in One's positive imagination.

Life#23

Don't discourage yourself with the arrangements of things; continuity is in the confusion of the arrangement.
A positive imagination leads to positive creativity.
One's imagination has no limitations.
"UNDERSTANDING"

Life#24

Be careful...
Expectations can make disappointments.
Sometimes reality is an illusion of
expectations riding in the express lane may
not be the safest way to travel..

Life#25

If One uses the rules for vowels. "It's I before
you and sometimes why One may miss
understanding One's Vow..

Life#26

Revenge is not a hall pass. The catalyst of
hatred is rooted in ignorance.

Life#27

History is a window that looks in many
directions. Until it finds the future it
consumes the stepping stones of man.

Life#28

When the Stewards take the capital for
holding it, they are thieves. Opportunists
have no life code because in their God they
trust. The placement of your holdings
should not be a sacrifice. Those who take
more than they give should be fed with a
long-handled spoon.

Life#29

A stone has many purposes. It's the patron
choice of its application.

Life#30

One must understand nothing is ever lost
until it is forgotten. Many things should be
forgiven and never forgotten. "MOVE ON"

Life#31

It is important how you pack your bags. Too many things in One's baggage can make it very hard to carry. If you lift it every day, it will become lighter.

Life#32

The influence of One's positive words can radiate the world.

Life#33

If we learn to see with our ears as well as our eyes it will give us a clearer understanding of people's motivation. Close your eyes and listen. Can you see the world now?

Life#34

The Big Bang is the limited Resources.

Life#35

Clearing the knots that tangle One's lines
will make the process more practical. If a
line brakes, tie another one. Most of the
time it's the ties, not the knots that hold
things together. Knowing the strength of
One's lines can deceive One's limitations.

Life#36

It's the tail of the beast that gives the world
adversities.
Once it sits down and respectfully
cooperates, living gets better.

Life#37

What One values the most, will be One's
greatest loss.
The greatest treasure One can possess is
love. It cannot be put into a bottle or
molded by hands. It's a gift that never
stops giving. It can cost One nothing, or
cost One everything.

Life#38

The prisoner asked, "What is One in for?"
The liberated replied, "I am here for life."
There are infinite reasons people imprison
themselves to find freedom.

Life#39

Wandering around in the wilderness One
may be lost, fearful or find One's self. It's
what One makes of what happens to them
that makes opportunities.

Life#40

Making a zero may seem like One has
failed. On the contrary, every marksman is
off centered before his center can be
engaged accurately. Understanding what
puts one off the mark and, adjusting the
aim will make success eminent. The zero
has no end.

Life#41

A righteous man cannot close his door to
his adversaries.
It's incomprehensive how integrity
extinguishes the fires of injustice. The
righteous will stand where the immorality
has fallen. It's a fool who takes a domestic
cat to a dogfight.

Life#42

Any man who indulges in his troubles will be
drunk with regrets.

Life#43

Anyone who knows their weaknesses
understands their strength. True power
cannot acknowledge itself, it must have
admirers.

Life#44

It's not the zoo that holds the animals; it's the animals that hold the zoo. Stand in line and get your tickets to the Animal Farm.
It's incomprehensible how compassion can extinguish the fire of injustice.

Life#45

An eye for an eye eventually leaves everybody blind.

Life#46

The closely bonded seedling is never up rooted in a storm. Its flexibility bends with the wind and the rain makes it greener. Physical force creates physical forces. The prisoner of injustice must keep hope alive. Justice is not incarcerated in a free world.

Life#47

Big talk

    Get away with
Outrageous

        Political boarders
Opportunity Stand

    Your
    Ground

Peace Maker
    Legalized
        Assassin
Don't avoid
    The Classic
Between the World & Me

Life#48

Cash is the heartbeat of justice. Money knows how to manipulate the law and make profits. The last gun fired did not have a trigger. No integrity has worldly rewards until it tastes the truth.

Life#49

Telling a lie gains another lie until the world knows better. The truth can be hard to handle; give respect to a lie by knowing the truth. The truth that ripens on the vine is much sweeter than the one that is picked before its time.

Life#50

The biggest fear power has is the containment of power that is out of its custody. It takes courage to help those who cannot help themselves. WAR is not the answer.

Love Convictions

Love#1

The sun gives energy.
>No Charge

The plants give clean air.
>No Charge

Our world is LOVE and, it never stops giving..

Love#2

What One values the most will be One's greatest loss.

The greatest treasure One can possess is love. It cannot be put into a bottle or molded by hands. It's a gift that never stops giving. It can cost One nothing, or cost One everything.

Love#3

Better seats will get One closer to the entertainment. It will not put One on stage. Divine love cannot be staged

Love#4

When One can travel without baggage then
One's heart can be truly free

Love#5

It's the small drops of water that flow the
streams into rivers and, the rivers greet the
oceans and the oceans greet our world. Once we
understand that every drop of love counts, we
can greet the world as one.

Love#6

Love must be sincere to withstand the evils of
temptation. The virtues of true love will bind
perfect unity. Those who envy your success
will try to separate the mortar from your
happiness.

Love#7

Love your enemies and do well with them and lend to them without expectation. Your rewards will be great. If, One separates One's self from worldly matters, One will not have worldly matters to contend with.

Love#8

The things that emulate a holiday do not make a holiday. Things are just things. Expression should be spontaneous without time or date. The celebration of Life# is a blessing. **True love has NO IMPURITES ... only sacrifices.**

Spiritual Convictions

Spiritual #1

Most of us drive our vehicle to our desired location. We fasten our seat belts and grab the steering wheel and we drive. Can you remember that terrible accident you passed on the express way? It might have been somewhere local. Most of the time we rubber neck the tragedy with relief, because it's not someone close to us or someone we are acquainted with. It could have been minutes or maybe seconds ahead of us. Did you take the time to think why them and not me? We witnessed a tragedy. You may think you are an excellent driver because you have been driving for years without an accident. The senseless man does not know; fools do not understand. Psalm 92:6 NIV. They are in God's hands. Let us pray up, as we buckle up, in our travels. It is senseless to think we have total control of our destination. God bless you and

HAPPY NEW YEAR!

Spiritual #2

Rejuvenating seeds require the right soil
and perfect light. The living root will
always FLOURISH when its needs are
met.

Spiritual #3

A man can live 40 days without food, and
a man can live 3 days without water, yet
a man cannot live one second without faith.
Destiny without faith has no end. A dreamer
without a dream has no beginning.

Spiritual #4

*Don't entangle bad energy into your
meditation. Meditation is a refreshment.*

Spiritual #5

Once we realize what's holding us
up, we will have no conception of
failure.

Spiritual #6

We are given many gifts. Everyone possesses the power beyond their imagination. I met a man who claims to be king of many nations.

Spiritual #7

Your greatest treasure is in the mirror.

Spiritual #8

If One remains loyal to what they believe in, One truly has the power of faith. Faith without hope has no belief. Hope without faith does not exist.

Spiritual #9

Darkness is compelled to light and light comprehends darkness. One must be the light to comprehend darkness.

Spiritual #10

What you perceive, you will receive if you
believe.

Spiritual #11

The continuity of your belief has a great
affect on your thoughts. If one keeps
collecting useless things, one will have
useless space.
The tangible things can be physically
moved. The things that are intangible can
occupy several dimensions. Free will is not
free.

Spiritual #12

The investment of One's desires can
overshadow .One's necessity. The truth is
the catalyst to salvation.

Spiritual #13

One who serves has the greatest rewards.

Spiritual #14

Give thanks... the breeze of passion blankets
our world. God has given us thresholds to
peace with **FAITH**

Spiritual #15

Living well is no accident. The spiritual,
mental and physical are one.

Spiritual #16

Total darkness will allow One to easily
accept the light.

Spiritual #17

It was the stars that guided the mariners.
It is the stars that give light to darkness.
It is the stars that guided the three wise
men. It is the stars that allow the
dreamer to **"HAVE A DREAM."**

Spiritual #18

If one perceives, One can believe.
Where One has been is where, One is
going. It is the moment of conception
that gives birth to the end.

Spiritual #19

If One builds with anger and vengeance,
One cannot expect **SERENITY.**

Spiritual #20

The silhouettes of desires can
compromise One's intentions.
There are bottom feeders and top feeders.
Some will tell lies to gain prestige and
throw rocks, and hide their hands. He who
holds his tongue for righteous sake has a
heart of gold.

Spiritual #21

The mind can be tortured by delusions.
The center of one's universe is in one's
mind. It's all about mind and matter.
Agony minds misery and misery loves
company. If one does not mind it will not
matter. When the mind has nothing to put
on, it will find PEACE.

Spiritual #22

Peace and harmony are in the center of
One's universe. The vitality to One's
consciousness is neither seen nor heard,
only felt. Every man has his own path to
travel. Whoever seeks peace will find
peace.

Spiritual #23

Man's philosophy tries to pocket its world's
resources. The values of a man's treasure
are weighted in his ideas. When he feels
the pain of his action he will respect what
little time he occupies in this expanding
universe. PEACE...be with you.

Spiritual #24

There is a 24-hour communication service where calls do not drop and the lines are never busy. There is no call roaming or waiting.
The only requirement listed is...YOU MUST HAVE FAITH as small as a mustard seed. One's humble acceptance makes living so much easier. DON'T GIVE UP BECAUSE YOU GOT THE HOOK UP.

Spiritual #25

Nobody knows the expiration date or their greatest challenge. Every day is a new day. We should treat it special because tomorrow has no promise and life has no do over and n o regret.

Spiritual #26

What are your thoughts when you awaken
from a deep slumber? A hypnotist may
hypnotize somebody with a suggestion and
induce them into a deep sleep. Some people
toss in their sleep and talk in their sleep as
well as walk in their sleep. Many people
have sleep apnea. When a man is in a coma
the doctors do not know how long his
patient will sleep. Some are known to be
brain dead. Let us not be spiritually dead.
The deepest sleep known to man is **DEATH**
and no hypnotist or doctor has the power of
life to raise the dead. However, our Father
can remove the stones in our lives and raise
us from our iniquities.

 "WE MUST ALL HAVE FAITH."

Spiritual #27

Anyone who lives with the word of God
should be an example on how to live
with one's brothers and sisters.
Be strong and courageous; One's
integrity will stand where the
immorality has fallen.

Spiritual #27

Controlling your tongue will give you strength over your adversary. Silence can extinguish a fire and forgiviness can relinquish it forever.

Spiritual #28

As metal sharpens metal every soldier should be able to sharpen each other's sword with the contingency of the Word.

Spiritual #29

If one can understand the angles of perception, one has the ability to see what others will not with the Word of God.

Spiritual #30

Infatuation is committed to lust, and lust is like dust. It floats everywhere until it becomes a dirty settlement of mindless pleasures.

Spiritual #31

A baby comes into the world naked, with no anticipation of setting goals. There are no worries, no contentions, and no fears. It moves because it is alive. Nothing stays the same.
There are always constant changes. Sometimes we must take a chance to make a change. Our faith is in the cosmos. If our hearts were like clouds, the world would be so much better.

Spiritual #32

We are emotional beings. Our cries are for numerous meaning when our needs are not met. Keep the faith and don't entangle bad energy into your meditation. Do your best. God will pave the way. Clarity can coagulate more ways than one.

Spiritual #33

Good seeds will not grow anywhere. A garden must have good seeds to flourish.

Spiritual #34

Time... will release any prisoner and faith will resurrect the dead.

Spiritual #35

Raising your voice will not make your pupil understand any better. The master lets his students capture knowledge in unspoken words of wisdom.

Spiritual #36

Cats and dogs are not expected to have good relationships. Contrary to One's belief, love and hate complement each other. WE ALL CAN GET ALONG with the Word of God.

Spiritual #37

Realism is a reflection of reality and reality is the perception of the believer.

Spiritual #38

The investment of one's desires can overshadow one's necessity. The truth is the catalyst to salvation.

Spiritual #39

Wandering around in the wilderness may seem lost. It is what one does with their time that complements their existence.

Spiritual #40

It is the transformation of disbelief to believe that gets the AWE... in awesome in the Word of God.

Spiritual #41

It's the parts of the puzzle that completes the picture and every part has its purpose.
Confusion shapes the probabilities. The truth is not hard to find when your heart is right.

Spiritual #42

It's the lips that allow the tongue to speak.
Render your words wisely, for every word
spoken unkindly has its consequences.
There are those who don't know how to stay
in their own lane. They will try to dissuade
your clarity. The door of opportunity is
always open. Let your virtues be the
receptionist.

Spiritual #43

I know an inexpensive insurance everyone
can afford. They do not care about where
you live or who you are. They have wind
insurance, house insurance, automotive
insurance, life insurance and death
insurance. It is satisfaction guaranteed.
The insurance will never drop you or leave
you. It has a 24-hour service. It has never
been bankrupt and it is the best insurance
known to man. The insurance is
JESUS...God's policies are inexpensive.
They are better than Allstate's
good hands and Citizen's umbrella.
Everybody should have full coverage.

Biography

Hamilton Walker is a third generation
descendant of share croppers. His parents
migrated from Georgia to Miami in search of
better economic opportunities. They
struggled with the rising cost of living in the
big city. It was difficult for them to raise a
family of six on minimum wages.
Hamilton finished high school and joined
the U.S. military to lighten the family
load. He is an Army and Air Force
veteran who spent many years serving
his country. An avid tennis player, he
does community service by mentoring
and teaching youth tennis.
His connections with the adversities of life
inspired him to write. It is essential for
him to write to his family and friends
about the challenges of life. He wishes not
to stand in the way or lead the way. He
realizes it takes a tremendous amount of
pressure and time to transform coal into
a diamond. He reflects by saying, "We are
all jewels under the pressures of life."

Once we realize we are one and press together we will become stronger than the hardest substance known to man.

My journeys seem very long when I measure my life by an hour glass. I would like to give thanks to my family who has made my journey manageable. There are many people to whom I am grateful. My wife, Sharon, is the corner stone in my life. I am also grateful to the following people: Leyla, Bertha, James and Vince, for reading and commenting on my manuscripts. They encourage me to write more.